KS1 Success

Age 5-7

English

SATs Practice Workbook

Practice Workbook

Helen Cooper

Contents

Reading

Writing

Punctuation

Grammar and Spelling

SATs Practice Questions

Glossary

Answers

Set in a separate booklet in the centre of the book

Phonics

1 Which word is the real word?

a. derk dark kark firk **(1 mark)**

...... dark ......

b. lult look lelt lalt **(1 mark)**

...... look ......

c. beach braich bloud bouck **(1 mark)**

...... beach ......

2 Which word is the nonsense word?

a. drink think thrunk drives **(1 mark)**

...... thrunk ......

b. shoe chrick shape cheek **(1 mark)**

...... chrick ......

c. creep coin croak crilm **(1 mark)**

...... crilm ......

Picture cues

1 Look at the photographs below.

a. <u>Underline</u> the words you think go with this photograph. **(2 marks)**

<u>forest</u>   traffic

<u>tree</u>   road

b. <u>Underline</u> the words you think go with this photograph. **(2 marks)**

shop   <u>sea</u>

house   <u>sand</u>

Context

1 Choose the correct word from the box to put into each sentence.

great	learn	and	tag

a. I would like to .....**learn**..... to play tag rugby. **(1 mark)**

b. It is a good game for boys .....**and**..... girls. **(1 mark)**

c. You have to wear a .....**tag**..... on your back. **(1 mark)**

d. It is a .....**great**..... way of exercising. **(1 mark)**

2 Fill in the missing words in the following passage. **(6 marks)**

enjoyed	learning	like	part	school	started

We .....**like**..... to play tag rugby at our .....**school**..... this year. At first I didn't think I would .....**like**..... it, but since I started .....**learning**..... to play, I have really .....**enjoyed**..... it. I think it is good to take .....**part**.....

in a team game.

Sentences make sense

Top tip! Use all the strategies you have learned when reading. This will help you to enjoy your reading more and make you a better reader!

1 Rewrite the words into sentences that make sense.

a. run have to fast. really You **(1 mark)**

.....You really have to run fast.....

b. pull tag. your Someone to tries **(1 mark)**

.....Someone tries to pull your tag.....

c. muddy. You get might very **(1 mark)**

.....You might get very muddy.....

d. speed skills. have to You your practise **(1 mark)**

.....You have to practise your speed skills.....

Total $\frac{24}{24}$

Characters

❶ Choose a character from the words below and write it under its matching description.

| an athlete | a new teacher | a new sort of animal |

a. It had a large round, hairy, brown body. Its head was shaped like an egg. It had three large horns and two large green eyes. **(1 mark)**

an new Sorr of animal

b. He was very tall and thin. His face was serious but his voice was soft and kind. His hands played with his sleeves as he spoke. I think he was as nervous as we were. **(1 mark)**

a new teacher ✓

c. Her muscles moved as she warmed up. She had strong, powerful legs and arms. She stared straight ahead, with a look of concentration on her face. **(1 mark)**

an Athlect ✓

Settings

❶ Write these words and phrases into the correct setting in the table. **(3 marks)** ✓✓✓

icy   freezing   vines   traffic   buildings   trees

green   snow   icebergs   sweaty   tarmac   cars

A Jungle	A City	The North Pole

Types of fiction

1 What kind of stories would start with these sentences?

an adventure story	a traditional tale	a fairy story

a. Once upon a time there were three billy goats gruff... **(1 mark)** ✓

....

b. Long, long ago in an enchanted castle, there lived a clever princess... **(1 mark)** ✓

...... A faeriy tale ......

c. Their bags were packed, their cars were ready. They were about to set off on the trip of their lives! **(1 mark)** ✓

...... A *nevencher story ......

Story book language

1 Which of the following options sound like story book language?
Tick (✓) each box. **(6 marks)**

And they all lived happily ever after. ☑ ✓

Write your name and the date. ☐

Once upon a time... ☑ ✓

Finally, put the cake tin in the oven. ☐

Long ago in a land faraway... ☑ ✓

I went to my uncle and aunt's house for tea. ☐

And he was never seen again! ☑ ✓

"Oh, what big teeth you've got!" ☑ ✓

There was once a scary dragon who lived in a deep, dark cave. ☑ ✓

Total 15

Types of non-fiction

1 Circle the different types of non-fiction. **(6 marks)**

a poem   a menu   a leaflet   a play

a traditional tale   a poster   an instruction leaflet

a website   a fairy story   information on packaging

2 a. Draw a line to match the glossary words to their definitions. **(4 marks)**

Word	Definition
a pizza	the bottom part of a pizza, made of dough
a pizza cutter	a solid food made from milk
base	a fast food, popular in Italy
cheese	a knife with a circular blade, specially for cutting pizza

b. Write a definition for these words.

i. Italy **(2 marks)**

a poulend fast food in Itily

ii. pasta **(2 marks)**

iii. a tomato **(2 marks)**

iv. herbs **(2 marks)**

Ordering instructions

1 Rewrite these instructions in the correct order and number them.　　**(6 marks)**

5 Put it in the oven to cook for 10 minutes.
1 First get the oven hot.
4 Put grated cheese on top of the tomato paste.
2 Next get a pizza base.
3 Spread tomato paste on the base.
5 Add other toppings you like.

....

....

....

....

....

....

Interpreting a non-fiction text

1 Look at this menu, then answer the questions.

> Cheese and tomato pizza..... £3
> Vegetable pizza £4
> Garlic bread.............................. £2
> Spicy tomato pasta £4.50
> Soft drinks............................£1.50

a. Which is the most expensive item?

.... **(1 mark)**

b. How much does the vegetable pizza cost?

........£4............................ **(1 mark)**

c. Which is the cheapest food on the menu? ....£1.50.............................**(1 mark)**

d. How much is a cheese and tomato pizza and a drink?　　**(1 mark)**

.....£4.50.........................

Total —
28

Rhyme

1 Add a rhyming word to each list.

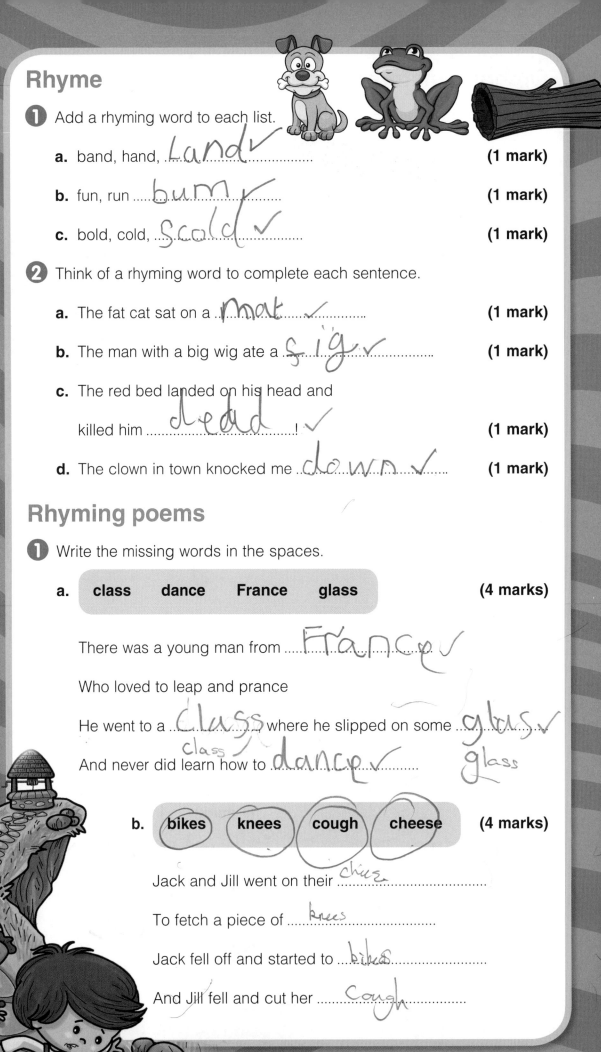

a. band, hand, ...land✓..... **(1 mark)**

b. fun, run .....bum✓..... **(1 mark)**

c. bold, cold, ...scold✓..... **(1 mark)**

2 Think of a rhyming word to complete each sentence.

a. The fat cat sat on a .....mat✓..... **(1 mark)**

b. The man with a big wig ate a .....fig✓..... **(1 mark)**

c. The red bed landed on his head and

killed him .....dead.....!✓ **(1 mark)**

d. The clown in town knocked me .....down✓..... **(1 mark)**

Rhyming poems

1 Write the missing words in the spaces.

a. | class | dance | France | glass | **(4 marks)**

There was a young man from .....France✓.....

Who loved to leap and prance

He went to a .....class.....where he slipped on some .....glass✓.....
class✓   glass

And never did learn how to .....dance✓.....

b. bikes   knees   cough   cheese **(4 marks)**

Jack and Jill went on their .....chus.....

To fetch a piece of .....knees.....

Jack fell off and started to .....bikes.....

And Jill fell and cut her .....cough.....

Alliteration

1 Make up some alliterative names for these people.
An example has been done for you.

Happy Helen

a. .... baby ✓ .... Ben **(1 mark)**

b. .... Sofia **(1 mark)**

c. .... Isaac **(1 mark)**

d. .... lapy ✓ .... Layla **(1 mark)**

2 Make up alliterative sentences using different letters.
The first one has been done for you.

Use letter l.

Lively Leo loves lemonade.

a. Use letter m. **(2 marks)**

Mooning murtle moans more. ✓

b. Use letter r. **(2 marks)**

Running tinosarans, rough, ralph. ✓

c. Use letter c. **(2 marks)**

Cats, crabs, click cat ✓

d. Use letter t. **(2 marks)**

the terrible tango turned tornado ✓

Total 27

Mixed-up sentences

1 Put the words in each sentence in the correct order.

a. I love the to zoo. going **(1 mark)**

I love going to the zoo.

b. animal is favourite My a zebra. **(1 mark)**

My favourite animal is a zebra

c. stripes. white love and black I their **(1 mark)**

d. house. bat bit I am scared a of the **(1 mark)**

e. laugh. penguins make The me **(1 mark)**

Missing words

1 Put these words in the correct places. **(9 marks)**

> hoop   afternoon   tricks   splashed   zookeeper
> fish   water   catch   sea lions

Every *afternoon* at four o'clock, the *zookeeper*
comes to feed the sea lions. She holds a *hoop fish*
up in the air and one of the *sealoins* jumps up to
catch it. Then she does it again for another sea lion.

When they have had enough fish, they do ....,

jumping through a .... If you stand too close

to the ...., you get ....!

Read and respond

Look at this sea lion fact file and answer the questions.

What it looks like	dark grey, ear flaps, four flippers, long front flippers and short, thick hair
Family	male sea lion – bull female – cow baby – pup
Food	lots of types of fish, squid, octopus
Where it lives	swims in water, sleeps on land
Movement	swims at about 11 miles per hour, although it can go as fast as 25 miles per hour walks on four flippers

1   **a.** How many flippers does a sea lion have? .... 4 ✓ .... (1 mark)

    b. Where does a sea lion sleep? .... Land ✓ .... (1 mark)

    c. What is the fastest a sea lion can swim? ...... 25 mph ...... (1 mark)

    d. Name two things that a sea lion eats. ...... fish Spid ✓ ...... (2 marks)

    e. What is the name given to a male sea lion? ...... bull ✓ ...... (1 mark)

2   Put a ✓ or a ✗ in each box.

    a. A female sea lion is called a pup.   ✗ ✓   (1 mark)

    b. Sea lions eat chips.   ✗ ✓   (1 mark)

    c. Some sea lions can swim up to 25 miles per hour.   ✓ ✓   (1 mark)

    d. Sea lions walk on their flippers.   ✓ ✓   (1 mark)

    e. A sea lion is green.   ✗ ✓   (1 mark)

Total 25

Deduction

1 Read the passage and then answer the questions.

> Sweat trickled down the back of his neck. The hot sun was beating down. Salty trails of sweat ran down his face. He looked at his friend. Her face was the colour of a red, ripe tomato. He wiggled his toes, which were hot and slippery in his sandals. "Phew! I wonder what the temperature is today," he said.

a. What is the weather like?   **(1 mark)**

....

b. Tick the phrases that tell you this: **(2 marks)**

the back of his neck ☐

The hot sun ☐

the colour of a red, ripe tomato ☐

wiggled his toes ☐

c. Why did he have salty trails running down his face?   **(1 mark)**

....

Inference

1 Read the passage below and then answer the questions.

> "I need a drink" he muttered crossly. He scowled when he saw Ava lift her water bottle to her lips and take a long drink. He began to jab at the hot sand with a stick. To his amazement, she did not offer him any, not even the smallest sip! She knew he had left his bottle on the rocks. He stood up and walked off in the direction of the rocks. "Are you ok?" called Ava, smiling at him. No he was not, he thought to himself angrily as he marched across the sand. How could anyone be so stupid?

a. What does the author want you to think the boy thinks about Ava? **(2 marks)**

....

....

b. What does the author want you to know about the boy? **(2 marks)**

....

....

c. How is the boy feeling? How can you tell? **(2 marks)**

....

....

Prediction

1 Read the passage below and then answer the question.

> The tide was coming in. As he got nearer to the rocks, he could see that the swirling water had covered the flat rock where he had left his bottle. It was gone. Hot tears filled his eyes. It was a twenty-minute walk back to the campsite. He was so thirsty and so hot. He turned and headed up the beach. Ava was standing by the path that led up to their tents, drinking from her bottle. "Please give me a drop," he said. "Oops, all gone," she said and giggled, as if she had just told a funny joke. He was furious.

What do you think might happen next? Think of two different ideas. **(4 marks)**

a. ....

....

b. ....

....

Total $\frac{}{14}$

Lower-case letters

Write the letters of the alphabet in lower-case, without joins.

Letters that sit on the line: **(1 mark)**

_____

Letters that stand tall on the line: **(1 mark)**

_____

Letters that hang their tails under the line: **(1 mark)**

_____

Upper-case letters

1 Write out all the letters of the alphabet in upper-case. **(2 marks)**

....

....

....

Cursive writing

1 Write all the letters of the alphabet in lower-case in the cursive style you have been learning. **(3 marks)**

....

....

....

Pangrams

1 Practise writing these sentences in your best handwriting.

a. The five boxing wizards jump quickly.   **(2 marks)**

....

....

b. The jay, pig, fox, zebra, monkey and wolves all quacked!   **(2 marks)**

....

....

....

c. A large fawn jumped quickly over white zinc boxes.   **(2 marks)**

....

....

....

d. Sixteen wonderful, valuable zigzag pots were quickly placed
into the sturdy jute bag.   **(2 marks)**

....

....

....

e. Crafty Frankie brought some amazing, exquisite pearl jewellery. **(2 marks)**

....

....

....

Total 18

Capital letters in a sentence

❶ Rewrite these sentences with a capital letter at the beginning.

a. i have a new baby sister. **(1 mark)**

....

b. we are going out to lunch today. **(1 mark)**

....

c. you can have an apple or a banana. **(1 mark)**

....

d. which way is it to the swimming pool? **(1 mark)**

....

When to use capital letters

❶ Write each word in its correct place in the table. **(12 marks)**

Saturday	April	Spain	Monday
September	Germany	Wednesday	March
New York	Friday	December	Paris

Places	Days of the Week	Months of the Year

Capital letters for names

1 Write these names with capital letters. **(8 marks)**

amelia	....
barney	....
chloe	....
dan	....
emily	....
francis	....
gabriel	....
helena	....

Adding capitals

1 Fill in the missing words choosing from the box below.
Don't forget the capital letters! **(7 marks)**

i cinderella december newcastle iris vincent tuesday

.... am a bit fed up. We have tickets to go to see "................................"

in .... We were going into .... to the theatre. My

friends, ... and ...., were coming with me.

On .... an email came to say that the show had been cancelled.

Total $\frac{}{31}$

Sloppy sentences

❶ Rewrite each sentence correctly.

a. where are the scissors I left on the table   **(2 marks)**

....

b. Let'sgoand pick some beans fromthegarden.   **(2 marks)**

....

c. My BROtheR says he is beTTer at climBing than me.   **(2 marks)**

....

....

d. Mysister and I hade grate funn onthe water slide.   **(2 marks)**

....

....

e. out teaCHer say wewill BE learning about the romans
necxt term   **(2 marks)**

....

....

Rearranging a recount

❶ Number the sentences 1–5 to put them in
an order that makes sense.   **(5 marks)**

| | When we got home we gave him a juicy bone, as a special treat.

| | Yesterday we went to a dog show.

| | We entered him into the competition for the dog with the waggiest tail.

| | He won first prize, a blue rosette!

| | We took our dog, Duke.

Story writing

① Draw a line to match each phrase to its type.　　　　**(6 marks)**

Once upon a time there was a fearsome dragon	plot
A huge, fiery dragon	beginning
A rocky canyon full of caves	middle
And he was never seen again	setting
The dragon wanted to rule over the kingdom	character
The brave princess set off to stop the dragon	end

Letter writing

① Write a short letter to someone thanking them for a birthday present.　　**(4 marks)**

Dear ....

....

....

....

....

Love from ....

Labelling a diagram

① Draw and label a diagram of your favourite toy. Use at least four labels.　　**(4 marks)**

Total —— 29

To plan or not to plan?

1 Which of these types of writing would you write a plan for?

Put a ✓ or a ✗ in each box.

a. a shopping list ☐ **(1 mark)**

b. a text message ☐ **(1 mark)**

c. a story ☐ **(1 mark)**

d. a poem ☐ **(1 mark)**

e. a recount ☐ **(1 mark)**

f. drawing and labelling a picture ☐ **(1 mark)**

g. a postcard ☐ **(1 mark)**

A story writing frame

1 Write a story plan for the traditional tale "The Little Red Hen". **(6 marks)**

Characters	
Setting	
Plot	
Intro/build up	
Conflict	
Resolution	

A non-fiction writing frame

1 Write a plan for a booklet about cats.   **(6 marks)**

Title	Facts About Cats
Sub-headings	
Ideas	
Vocabulary	

Drafts

1 Look at this first draft of a story. Rewrite it, firstly correcting the punctuation. Then change the adjective "nice" each time it appears, inserting another suitable adjective.   **(7 marks)**

> The children were having a nice time. It was a nice sunny day they were having a nice picnic in the woods. They had packed sandwiches fruit crisps cake and drinks. What an adventure it promised to be as they sat near the river, they saw an object in the water.

....

....

....

....

....

....

Total ─── 26

Writing in the present tense

1 Write a sentence using each verb in the present tense.

a. write **(2 marks)**

....

....

b. sing **(2 marks)**

....

....

c. cry **(2 marks)**

....

....

Writing in the present progressive

1 Use the verb "to be" + ing, e.g. **is** runn**ing**. Look at the pictures and use these verbs to finish the sentences.

> **saw**   **drill**

a. He is .... a piece of wood. **(1 mark)**

b. We are .... holes in the wall to put up a shelf. **(1 mark)**

2 Use these verbs to write your own sentences in the present progressive. The first one has been done for you. **(4 marks)**

> **fly**   **scream**   **help**

a. I am flying to Madrid tomorrow. ....

b. ....

c. ....

Writing in the past tense

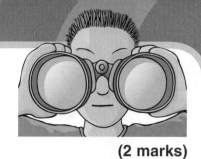

1 Write a sentence using each verb in the past tense.

a. watch   (2 marks)

....

....

b. sort   (2 marks)

....

....

c. slam   (2 marks)

....

....

Writing in the past progressive

1 Use the verb "to be" + ing, e.g. **was** walk**ing**.
Use these verbs to finish the sentences.

| colour   help |

a. I was .... a picture.   (1 mark)

b. She was .... her mum.   (1 mark)

2 Use these verbs to write your own sentences in the past progressive.
The first one has been done for you.   (4 marks)

| search   look   play |

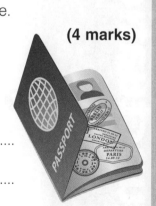

a. I was searching for my passport...

b. ....

c. ....

Total
24

Question marks

❶ Punctuate these sentences with a question mark.

a. Where are the scissors   **(1 mark)**

b. Can you come to my house to play on Saturday   **(1 mark)**

c. Is it going to rain today   **(1 mark)**

d. How many times have you been trampolining   **(1 mark)**

❷ Use these question words to complete these questions.

Which	Who	How	When

a. .... would like to go swimming?   **(1 mark)**

b. .... are your grandparents arriving?   **(1 mark)**

c. .... many cousins do you have?   **(1 mark)**

d. .... jumper do you like best?   **(1 mark)**

Exclamation marks and full stops

❶ Punctuate these sentences with either
an exclamation mark (**!**) or a full stop (**.**).

a. How good it will be at Zac's birthday party   **(1 mark)**

b. I have bought him a remote-controlled car   **(1 mark)**

c. What an amazing present he will think it is   **(1 mark)**

d. My dad says we need to find a big open space outside
to try it out   **(1 mark)**

❷ Are these sentences correctly punctuated? Write **yes** or **no**.

a. Do you have porridge for your breakfast
every day? ....   **(1 mark)**

b. What a funny thing I have seen! ....   **(1 mark)**

c. We wear a red school uniform. ....   **(1 mark)**

d. We laughed until our sides were hurting? ....   **(1 mark)**

Match the punctuation

1 Draw a line to match each sentence to its punctuation.

(6 marks)

What time does the show start	.
We can have popcorn during the show	!
Have you brought any water	.
What a brilliant day it was	?
How fantastic he is	?
I need to go to the toilet	!

Punctuate this passage

1 Put the correct punctuation marks in the passage below.

(7 marks)

The capital letters have been done for you.

Mum has been promising to take us to a show for ages Today we went to the theatre to see a show about a circus What incredible acrobats there were They wrapped themselves in red sheets hanging from the ceiling and did all sorts of moves How do they do them My sister and I tried to copy them when we got home All that happened was that we got our bed sheets tangled and mum was cross

Punctuation can make a difference to what your writing means. Choose carefully whether you think a full stop or an exclamation mark would be best.

Top tip!

Total 29

Sentences make sense

❶ Draw lines to match the two halves of these sentences. **(4 marks)**

a. | I would like to go | you'll never have enough money.

b. | Start saving now or | to Australia on holiday.

c. | Do you know how long | snorkel on the Great Barrier Reef!

d. | How brilliant it would be to | it takes to fly there?

Questions and statements

❶ Write a question for each of these statements.

a. The train leaves at 7 o'clock. **(1 mark)**

....

b. It arrives in Newcastle at 9 o'clock. **(1 mark)**

....

c. I bought a ticket yesterday. **(1 mark)**

....

❷ Write a statement for each of these questions.

a. How many stops does the train make? **(1 mark)**

....

b. Is there a shop on board? **(1 mark)**

....

c. Is there somewhere to leave my suitcase? **(1 mark)**

....

READING

Reading strategies

pages 4–5 Phonics

1 a. dark   **(1 mark)**   b. look   **(1 mark)**
   c. beach   **(1 mark)**

2 a. thrunk **(1 mark)**   b. chrick **(1 mark)**
   c. crilm   **(1 mark)**

Picture cues

1 a. <u>forest</u> **(1 mark)**   <u>tree</u> **(1 mark)**
   b. <u>sand</u>   **(1 mark)**   <u>sea</u> **(1 mark)**

Context

1 a. learn **(1 mark)**   b. and   **(1 mark)**
   c. tag   **(1 mark)**   d. great **(1 mark)**

2 We **started (1 mark)** to play tag rugby at our
   school (1 mark) this year. At first I didn't think
   I would **like (1 mark)** it, but since I started
   learning (1 mark) to play, I have really **enjoyed
   (1 mark)** it. I think it is good to take **part (1 mark)**
   in a team game.

Sentences make sense

1 a. You have to run really fast.   **(1 mark)**
   b. Someone tries to pull your tag.   **(1 mark)**
   c. You might get very muddy.   **(1 mark)**
   d. You have to practise your
      speed skills.   **(1 mark)**

Fiction

pages 6–7 Characters

1 a. a new sort of animal   **(1 mark)**
   b. a new teacher   **(1 mark)**
   c. an athlete   **(1 mark)**

Settings

1 A Jungle – vines, trees, green, sweaty **(1 mark)**
   A City – traffic, buildings, tarmac,
            cars   **(1 mark)**
   The North Pole – icy, freezing, snow,
                    icebergs   **(1 mark)**

**Note: sweaty/icy/freezing are all weather words
that would also be acceptable in describing a city.**

Types of fiction

1 a. a traditional tale   **(1 mark)**
   b. a fairy story   **(1 mark)**
   c. an adventure story   **(1 mark)**

Story book language

And they all lived happily
ever after.   ✓ **(1 mark)**
Once upon a time...   ✓ **(1 mark)**
Long ago in a land faraway...   ✓ **(1 mark)**
And he was never seen again!   ✓ **(1 mark)**
"Oh, what big teeth you've got!"   ✓ **(1 mark)**
There was once a scary dragon
who lived in a deep, dark cave.   ✓ **(1 mark)**

Non-fiction

pages 8–9 Types of non-fiction

1 (a menu)**(1 mark)** (a leaflet)**(1 mark)**
   (a poster)**(1 mark)** (an instruction leaflet)**(1 mark)**
   (a website)**(1 mark)** (information on packaging)
                                          (1 mark)

2 a. a pizza ⟶ a fast food, popular in Italy
      a pizza cutter ⟶ a knife with a circular
         blade, specially for cutting pizza
      base ⟶ the bottom part of a pizza,
         made of dough
      cheese ⟶ a solid food made from milk
                                          (4 marks)
   b. i.   Italy – a country in Europe   **(2 marks)**
      ii. pasta – a food like spaghetti; it can
           come in lots of different shapes   **(2 marks)**
      iii. a tomato – a red fruit that can be
           eaten raw or cooked   **(2 marks)**
      iv. herbs – plants used in cooking to
           add flavour to food   **(2 marks)**

**Accept answers that are similar to these.
(2 marks: 1 mark for a short answer, extra mark
for more detail)**

Ordering instructions

1 1. First get the oven hot.   **(1 mark)**
   2. Next get a pizza base.   **(1 mark)**
   3. Spread tomato paste on the base.   **(1 mark)**
   4. Put grated cheese on top of the
      tomato paste.   **(1 mark)**
   5. Add other toppings you like.   **(1 mark)**
   6. Put it in the oven to cook for
      10 minutes.   **(1 mark)**

Interpreting a non-fiction text

1 a. spicy tomato pasta   **(1 mark)**
   b. £4   **(1 mark)**
   c. garlic bread   **(1 mark)**
   d. £4.50   **(1 mark)**

Poetry

pages 10–11 Rhyme

1 a. A word ending -and, e.g. land   **(1 mark)**
   b. A word ending -un, e.g. bun   **(1 mark)**
   c. A word ending -old, e.g. sold   **(1 mark)**

2 a. A word ending -at which will
      make sense, e.g. mat   **(1 mark)**
   b. A word ending -ig which will
      make sense, e.g. fig   **(1 mark)**
   c. A word ending -ed which will
      make sense, e.g. dead   **(1 mark)**
   d. A word ending -own which
      will make sense, e.g. down   **(1 mark)**

Rhyming poems

1 a. France **(1 mark)**   class **(1 mark)**
      glass **(1 mark)**   dance **(1 mark)**
   b. bikes **(1 mark)**   cheese **(1 mark)**

cough **(1 mark)**   knees **(1 mark)**

Alliteration

1 a. **Accept an adjective that begins with B**, e.g. Brilliant Ben   **(1 mark)**
   b. **Accept an adjective that begins with S**, e.g. Sleepy Sofia   **(1 mark)**
   c. **Accept an adjective that begins with I**, e.g. Idle Isaac   **(1 mark)**
   d. **Accept an adjective that begins with L,** e.g. Lazy Layla   **(1 mark)**

2 a. Accept a **sentence using mostly words beginning with m**, e.g. Marvellous Marigold makes marmalade.
   b. Accept a **sentence using mostly words beginning with r**, e.g. Ruthless Richard runs in the rain.
   c. Accept a **sentence using mostly words beginning with c**, e.g. Clever Colin collects coins.
   d. Accept a **sentence using mostly words beginning with t**, e.g. Tall trees tower above Tim.

(2 marks: 1 mark for a couple of alliterative words, an extra mark for more alliterative words)

Comprehension

pages 12–13 Mixed up sentences.

1 a. I love going to the zoo.   **(1 mark)**
   b. My favourite animal is a zebra.   **(1 mark)**
   c. I love their black and white stripes.   **(1 mark)**
   d. I am a bit scared of the bat house.   **(1 mark)**
   e. The penguins make me laugh.   **(1 mark)**

Missing words

1 afternoon, zookeeper, fish, sea lions, catch, tricks, hoop, water, splashed   **(9 marks)**

Read and respond

1 a. four   **(1 mark)**
   b. on the land   **(1 mark)**
   c. 25 miles per hour   **(1 mark)**
   d. Two from: squid, fish, octopus   **(1 mark)**
   e. bull   **(1 mark)**

2 a. ✗ b. ✗ c. ✓ d. ✓ e. ✗   **(5 marks)**

More comprehension skills

pages 14–15 Deduction

1 a. hot, sunny   **(1 mark)**
   b. The hot sun ✓   **(1 mark)**
      the colour of a red, ripe tomato ✓   **(1 mark)**
   c. He was sweating   **(1 mark)**

Inference

1 a. **Accept answers along the lines of:** The author wants you to think that the boy thinks that she is thoughtless or unkind, that she is not a nice person. **(2 marks: 1 for one reason, an extra mark for more)**
   b. **Accept answers along the lines of:** The author wants you to know that he is being

bad tempered and very angry with Ava or cross with himself for leaving his water bottle behind. **(2 marks: 1 for one reason, an extra mark for more)**
   c. The boy is angry. The author describes the boy using words like muttered crossly, scowled, jab, to his amazement, angrily, so stupid, to show us how he is feeling. **(2 marks: 1 for one reason, an extra mark for more)**

Prediction

1 **Accept any suitable answers**, e.g.
   a. The boy cries and runs off to the campsite leaving Ava.
   b. Ava sees the boy is upset and says sorry.

WRITING

Handwriting

pages 16–17 Lower case letters

1 Letters that sit on the line:
   aceimnorsuvwxz   **(1 mark)**
   Letters that stand tall on the line: bdfhklt **(1 mark)**
   Letters that hang their tails under the line:
   gjpqy   **(1 mark)**

Upper case letters

1 ABCDEFGHIJKLMNOPQRSTUVWXYZ **(2 marks)**

Cursive writing

1 Check your child's writing. **(3 marks for all letters correctly formed)**

Pangrams

1 Check your child's writing. **(10 marks: 2 marks for each sentence correctly written)**

Capital letters

pages 18–19 Capital letters in a sentence

1 a. **I** have a new baby sister.   **(1 mark)**
   b. **W**e are going out to lunch today.   **(1 mark)**
   c. **Y**ou can have an apple or a banana. **(1 mark)**
   d. **W**hich way is it to the swimming pool? **(1 mark)**

When to use capital letters

1 **Places** – Spain, Germany, New York, Paris   **(4 marks)**

   Days of the Week – Saturday, Monday, Wednesday, Friday   **(4 marks)**

   Months of the Year – April, September, March, December   **(4 marks)**

Capital letters for names

1 Amelia **(1 mark)**   Barney **(1 mark)**
   Chloe **(1 mark)**   Dan **(1 mark)**   Emily **(1 mark)**
   Francis **(1 mark)**   Gabriel **(1 mark)**
   Helena **(1 mark)**

Adding capitals

1 **I** **(1 mark)** am a bit fed up. We have tickets to go to see "**Cinderella**" **(1 mark)** in **December**. **(1 mark)** We were going into **Newcastle** **(1 mark)**

to the theatre. My friends, **Iris (1 mark)** and **Vincent (1 mark)**, were coming with me. On **Tuesday (1 mark)** an email came to say that the show had been cancelled. **(Accept Iris and Vincent in either order)**

Features of writing
pages 20–21 Sloppy sentences
1 a. Where are the scissors I left on the table? **(2 marks)**
   b. Let's go and pick some beans from the garden. **(2 marks)**
   c. My brother says he is better at climbing than me. **(2 marks)**
   d. My sister and I had great fun on the water slide. **(2 marks)**
   e. Our teacher says we will be learning about the Romans next term. **(2 marks)**

Rearranging a recount
1 1. Yesterday we went to a dog show. **(1 mark)**
   2. We took our dog, Duke. **(1 mark)**
   3. We entered him into the competition for the dog with the waggiest tail. **(1 mark)**
   4. He won first prize, a blue rosette! **(1 mark)**
   5. When we got home we gave him a juicy bone, as a special treat. **(1 mark)**

Story writing

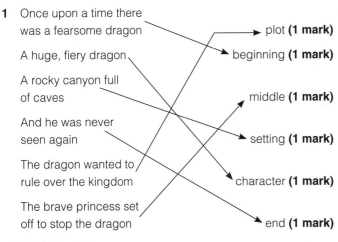

1 Once upon a time there was a fearsome dragon → plot **(1 mark)**

A huge, fiery dragon → beginning **(1 mark)**

A rocky canyon full of caves → middle **(1 mark)**

And he was never seen again → setting **(1 mark)**

The dragon wanted to rule over the kingdom → character **(1 mark)**

The brave princess set off to stop the dragon → end **(1 mark)**

Letter writing
1 This is an example of what the letter might look like:

Dear Amba,

   Thank you for my paints and sketch pad. They are fantastic! I will practise some drawing and painting with them this afternoon.

                    Love from Libby **(4 marks)**

Labelling a diagram
Award **4 marks** for a drawing labelled with the names of **four** different parts of the toy.
For example:

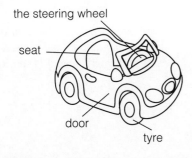

the steering wheel

seat

door

tyre

Planning and checking
pages 22–23 To plan or not to plan?
1 a. ☒ **(1 mark)** b. ☒ **(1 mark)**
  c. ☑ **(1 mark)** d. ☑ **(1 mark)**
  e. ☑ **(1 mark)** f. ☒ **(1 mark)**
  g. ☒ **(1 mark)**

A story writing frame
1 This is an example of how the story plan might look:

Characters	Little Red Hen dog cat	**(1 mark)**
Setting	farm fields mill	**(1 mark)**
Plot	Hen wants to make a loaf of bread.	**(1 mark)**
Intro/build up	Hen sows corn. Asks friends to help reap.	**(1 mark)**
Conflict	Friends won't help thresh/ grind/cook/bake.	**(1 mark)**
Resolution	Hen makes a loaf and eats it herself.	**(1 mark)**

A non-fiction writing frame
1 This is an example of how the writing frame might look:

Title	Facts About Cats
Sub-headings	What does a cat look like? What do cats eat? How do cats behave? Where do cats sleep? **(2 marks)**
Ideas	draw and label a picture of a cat eat – spider diagram behaviour – list sleep – photos of different cat baskets **(2 marks)**
Vocabulary	cat, claws, whiskers, diet **(2 marks)**

Drafts
1 This is an example of how an amended first draft might look:

The children were having a **wonderful** time. It was a **hot,** sunny day**. They** were having a **delicious** picnic in the woods. They had packed sandwiches, fruit, crisps, cake and drinks. What an adventure it promised to be**! As** they sat near the river, they saw an object in the water.

(7 marks)

Using verbs in writing
pages 24–25 Writing in the present tense
1 a. A sentence using the verb **write** in the present tense correctly, e.g. I write five letters every day. **(2 marks)**
   b. A sentence using the verb **sing** in the present tense correctly, e.g. You sing your favourite song. **(2 marks)**
   c. A sentence using the verb **cry** in the present tense correctly, e.g. She cries because she has lost her purse. **(2 marks)**

Writing in the present progressive

1. a. He is **sawing** a piece of wood. **(1 mark)**
   b. We are **drilling** holes in the wall to put up a shelf. **(1 mark)**

2. b. Accept any suitable sentence using the word **screaming**, e.g. She is screaming in delight on the fairground ride. **(2 marks)**
   c. Accept any suitable sentence using the word **helping**, e.g. He is helping his mother in the kitchen. **(2 marks)**

Writing in the past tense

1. a. A sentence using the word **watch** in the past tense correctly, e.g. I watched a cartoon yesterday. **(2 marks)**
   b. A sentence using the word **sort** in the past tense correctly, e.g. He sorted the pound coins into a pile. **(2 marks)**
   c. A sentence using the word **slam** in the past tense correctly, e.g. You slammed the door. **(2 marks)**

Writing in the past progressive

1. a. I was **colouring** a picture. **(1 mark)**
   b. She was **helping** her mum. **(1 mark)**

2. b. Accept any suitable sentence using the word **looking**, e.g. The boy was looking for this ball. **(2 marks)**
   c. Accept any suitable sentence using the word **playing**, e.g. The girl was playing with her paints. **(2 marks)**

PUNCTUATION

Finding punctuation marks

pages 26–27 Question marks

1. a. Where are the scissors**?** **(1 mark)**
   b. Can you come to my house to play on Saturday**?** **(1 mark)**
   c. Is it going to rain today**?** **(1 mark)**
   d. How many times have you been trampolining**?** **(1 mark)**

2. a. Who **(1 mark)** b. When **(1 mark)**
   c. How **(1 mark)** d. Which **(1 mark)**

Exclamation marks and full stops

1. a. How good it will be at Zac's birthday party**!** **(1 mark)**
   b. I have bought him a remote controlled car**.** **(1 mark)**
   c. What an amazing present he will think it is**!** **(1 mark)**
   d. My dad says we need to find a big open space outside to try it out**.** **(1 mark)**

2. a. yes **(1 mark)** b. yes **(1 mark)**
   c. yes **(1 mark)** d. no **(1 mark)**

Match the punctuation

1. What time does the show start   . **(1 mark)**
   We can have popcorn during the show   ! **(1 mark)**
   Have you brought any water   . **(1 mark)**
   What a brilliant day it was   ? **(1 mark)**
   How fantastic he is   ? **(1 mark)**
   I need to go to the toilet   ! **(1 mark)**

Punctuate this passage

1. Mum has been promising to take us to a show for ages**. (1 mark)** Today we went to the theatre to see a show about a circus**. (1 mark)** What incredible acrobats there were**! (1 mark)** They wrapped themselves in red sheets hanging from the ceiling and did all sorts of moves**. (1 mark)** How do they do them**? (1 mark)** My sister and I tried to copy them when we got home**. (1 mark)** All that happened was that we got our bed sheets tangled and mum was cross**. (1 mark)**

Different types of sentences

pages 28–29 Sentences make sense

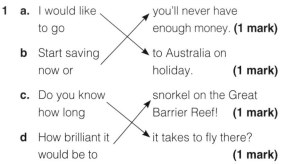

1. a. I would like to go — you'll never have enough money. **(1 mark)**
   b Start saving now or — to Australia on holiday. **(1 mark)**
   c. Do you know how long — snorkel on the Great Barrier Reef! **(1 mark)**
   d How brilliant it would be to — it takes to fly there? **(1 mark)**

Questions and statements

1. Answers should be similar to these examples.
   a. What time does the train leave? **(1 mark)**
   b. What time does the train arrive? **(1 mark)**
   c. When did you buy a ticket? **(1 mark)**

2. Answers should be similar to these examples.
   a. The train stops six times. **(1 mark)**
   b. There is a shop on board. **(1 mark)**
   c. There is a luggage rack for your suitcase. **(1 mark)**

Commands and exclamations

1. **Commands**

Choose a book. **(1 mark)**
Get your coat. **(1 mark)**
Pay at the till. **(1 mark)**

Exclamations

What a goal he scored! **(1 mark)**
How awesome that was! **(1 mark)**
What a panic it caused! **(1 mark)**

Which is which?

1   Who is that? – question   **(1 mark)**
    I think it's Zachary. – statement   **(1 mark)**
    Pass me my glasses. – command   **(1 mark)**
    How good you are! – exclamation   **(1 mark)**

Commas

pages 30–31 Commas in lists

1 **a.** School days: Monday, Tuesday, Wednesday,
       Thursday, Friday   **(1 mark)**
   b. Seasons of the year: spring, summer,
       autumn, winter   **(1 mark)**
   c. Months in autumn: September,
       October, November   **(1 mark)**

2 **a.** Things in a bedroom: a bed, a wardrobe, a chest of
       drawers, a lamp
   b. Things in a bathroom: a shower, a bath, a toilet, a towel
   c. Things in a kitchen: a fridge, a washing machine,
       a cooker, a kettle

(2 marks: 1 for correctly sorting the list, 1 for the commas in the correct place)

Lists within sentences

1 **a.** In my grandma's garden there is a pond,
       a shed, a bench and lots of beautiful flowers. **(1 mark)**
   b. My granddad likes to go for walks, watch
       television, read books and play with me. **(1 mark)**
   c. My mum likes swimming, reading,
       travelling and going to the theatre. **(1 mark)**
   d. My dad likes hiking, reading, watching
       films and going out with his friends. **(1 mark)**

Writing sentences using commas

1 Accept suitable sentences similar to these examples.
   a. Today I am wearing a coat, a hat, a scarf and some
      gloves.
   b. I am taking my pyjamas, a dressing gown, slippers and
      my toothbrush to my cousin's house.
   c. At the safari park I saw lions, giraffes, zebras and
      hippos.

(2 marks: 1 for sentence structure, 1 for correct use of commas)

2 Accept suitable sentences with commas used correctly, for example:
   a. Last summer we went to the theatre, the zoo, a funfair
      and the park.
   b. My favourite foods are fish and chips, sausages, tomato
      soup and chocolate cake.
   c. My friend has a cat, a rabbit and a guinea pig.

(2 marks: 1 for sentence structure, 1 for correct use of commas)

Apostrophes for contractions

pages 32–33 Forming contractions

1 it's **(1 mark)** we're **(1 mark)** she'd **(1 mark)**
   can't **(1 mark)** we'll **(1 mark)** doesn't **(1 mark)**
   don't **(1 mark)** hadn't **(1 mark)** would've **(1 mark)**
   couldn't **(1 mark)** you're **(1 mark)** he'd **(1 mark)**
   you'll **(1 mark)** we've **(1 mark)**

Sentences with contractions

1 **a.** I'm or You're **(1 mark)**   **b.** you'll **(1 mark)**
   c. can't **(1 mark)**   **d.** You're or I'm **(1 mark)**
   e. Don't **(1 mark)**

Contractions in writing

1 **a.** I'm **(1 mark)** **b.** I've **(1 mark)** **c.** we're **(1 mark)**
   d. we've **(1 mark)** **e.** we'll **(1 mark)** **f.** you'll **(1 mark)**
   g. would've **(1 mark)** **h.** couldn't **(1 mark)**

2

Dear Mr Goofy,

    You have (1 mark) an appointment booked with the dentist on Monday 31st October. **He will (1 mark)** give you a check-up and tell you if there are any problems. **You will (1 mark)** be charged a fee of £15.00 for your visit. Please **do not (1 mark)** forget to tell us if you **cannot (1 mark)** come to the appointment, otherwise **we shall (accept will) (1 mark)** have to charge you a cancellation fee.

Yours sincerely,
Mr C Dracula (Dental Receptionist)

Apostrophes for belonging

pages 34–35 Apostrophes for belonging

1 **b.** The baby's rattle   **(1 mark)**
   c. The cat's whiskers   **(1 mark)**
   d. The butterfly's wings   **(1 mark)**
   e. The kite's tail   **(1 mark)**
   f. The doll's ribbon   **(1 mark)**

Yes or no?

1 **a.** yes **(1 mark)**   **b.** no **(1 mark)**   **c.** yes **(1 mark)**
   d. no **(1 mark)**   **e.** no **(1 mark)**   **f.** yes **(1 mark)**

What's missing?

1 **a.** Amber's dresses   **(1 mark)**
   b. Sally's flowers   **(1 mark)**
   c. The boy's shirt   **(1 mark)**
   d. The girl's skirt   **(1 mark)**
   e. Jess's jumper   **(1 mark)**
   f. Sean's scooter   **(1 mark)**

Sentences with apostrophes

1 Accept suitable sentences showing the correct use of the apostrophe, e.g.
   a. Evie's hair is as white as snow.
   b. Annie's guitar does not get used very often.
   c. Nathan's computer is in the corner of the family room.
   d. Thomas's hockey stick got left behind on the field after
      the game.

(2 marks: 1 for sentence structure, 1 for correct use of apostrophes)

2 **a.** ✗ No apostrophe needed on photos.   **(1 mark)**
   b. ✗ Should be Karl's   **(1 mark)**
   c. ✗ No apostrophe needed on
      sandals.   **(1 mark)**
   d. ✓   **(1 mark)**

Answers

GRAMMAR AND SPELLING

Conjunctions

pages 36–37 Joining sentences

1 a. but   **(1 mark)** b. because **(1 mark)**
   c. and   **(1 mark)** d. and   **(1 mark)**

Using conjunctions

1 Accept any suitable endings, e.g.
   a. Henry worked hard and
      received top marks. **(1 mark)**
   b. It is late but I am still going
      out to play. **(1 mark)**
   c. They went into town because they
      wanted to buy some books. **(1 mark)**
   d. Ruby has been saving her money
      because she wants to go on holiday. **(1 mark)**

Choosing conjunctions

1 a. because/when **(1 mark)**
   b. but/when   **(1 mark)**
   c. because   **(1 mark)**
   d. that   **(1 mark)**
   e. or   **(1 mark)**

Co-ordinating or subordinating?

1 a. co-ordinating **(1 mark)**
   b. co-ordinating **(1 mark)**
   c. subordinating **(1 mark)**
   d. subordinating **(1 mark)**

Word classes

pages 38–39 Nouns

1 **Cutlery** – fork, spoon
   Clothing – shorts, trainers
   Art equipment – palette, paintbrush
(1 mark for each complete correct set of 2)

2 **Nouns** – king, cheese
   Proper nouns – Greece, Shola
(1 mark per correct set)

Adjectives

1 a. The sugary **(1 mark)** cake smelled
      so sweet! **(1 mark)**
   b. The sticky **(1 mark)** glue was all over
      the table.
   c. The excited **(1 mark)** children ran around the
      crowded **(1 mark)** playground.

2 Accept any suitable adjectives, e.g.
   a. The **keen (1 mark)** teacher waited at the
      classroom door.
   b. Our dog has **brown (1 mark)** fur and a **long
      (1 mark)** tail.
   c. There was a **loud (1 mark)** bang and the
      room went dark!

Adverbs

1 a. gracefully **(1 mark)** b. smoothly **(1 mark)**
   c. quickly **(1 mark)** d. athletically **(1 mark)**

2 Accept any three suitable adverbs e.g.:
   a. walk – quickly, **(1 mark)** slowly, **(1 mark)**
      silently **(1 mark)**

   b. jump – happily, **(1 mark)** smoothly, **(1 mark)**
      athletically **(1 mark)**
   c. sing – quietly, **(1 mark)** cheerfully, **(1 mark)**
      beautifully **(1 mark)**
   d. shout – angrily, **(1 mark)** loudly, **(1 mark)**
      aggressively **(1 mark)**

Verbs

1 loved **(1 mark)** told **(1 mark)**
   to bake **(1 mark)** washed up **(1 mark)**
   took **(1 mark)** tidied **(1 mark)**
   chose **(1 mark)** went **(1 mark)**
   to bake **(1 mark)** was trying **(1 mark)**
   collected **(1 mark)** to make **(1 mark)**
   gathered **(1 mark)** looked **(1 mark)**
   started **(1 mark)**
   remembered **(1 mark)**

Noun phrases

pages 40–41 Identifying noun phrases

1 a. The giant wore huge, clumpy boots. **(1 mark)**
   b. He had a tangled, messy beard. **(1 mark)**
   c. He had an enormous belly. **(1 mark)**
   d. His fingers were part of his huge,
      hairy hands. **(1 mark)**
   e. His voice boomed like a big
      bass drum. **(1 mark)**
   f. Spit dribbled from his large,
      wobbly lips. **(1 mark)**

Expanded noun phrases

1 Accept any complete sentences that make
   sense, e.g.
   a. **I put bread out for** the little bird that
      landed on the bird table. **(2 marks)**
   b. The screaming child who fell
      off the climbing frame
      needed a plaster. **(2 marks)**
   c. The tall boy with the curly hair **went to
      the hairdressers to have a haircut. (2 marks)**
   d. **I was jealous of** the little girl with the
      big, red bag. **(2 marks)**

Writing noun phrases

1 Accept any suitable answer that uses one or
   two adjectives, e.g.
   b. a **sleek, black** cat **(1 mark)**
   c. an **old, wooden** chair **(1 mark)**
   d. a **sharp, red** pencil **(1 mark)**
   e. a **wet, colourful** surfboard **(1 mark)**

Writing expanded noun phrases

1 Accept a noun phrase that uses one or two
   adjectives, plus a bit more detail, e.g.
   a. a big, round ball on the pavement **(2 marks)**
   b. a red hula hoop in the shed **(2 marks)**
   c. a rusty bicycle owned by the boy **(2 marks)**
   d. an old teddy bear that the girl loved **(2 marks)**

Past and present tenses

pages 42–43 The present tense

1 a. [✗] She **likes** reading.   (1 mark)

  b. I cook great pancakes! [✓]   (1 mark)

  c. They play hopscotch. [✓]   (1 mark)

  d. [✗] We **think** our teacher is very funny.   (1 mark)

The past tense

1 a. I **watched** a great film yesterday.   (1 mark)

  b. He **jumped** as high as he could on
       the trampoline.   (1 mark)

  c. We **laughed** at Isaac's joke.   (1 mark)

  d. She **shouted** across the room.   (1 mark)

  e. They **walked** quickly into the party.   (1 mark)

2 Accept any suitable answer that uses
   the verb correctly, e.g.

  a. We kicked a ball around.   (1 mark)

  b. Dad cooked dinner last night.   (1 mark)

  c. I talked to my sister on the phone.   (1 mark)

  d. She planted onions in her garden.   (1 mark)

–ing endings

1 a. jump + ing = jumping   (1 mark)

  b. water + ing = watering   (1 mark)

  c. grow + ing = growing   (1 mark)

  d. play + ing = playing   (1 mark)

  e. ride + ing = riding   (1 mark)

  f. drive + ing = driving   (1 mark)

  g. like + ing = liking   (1 mark)

  h. chase + ing = chasing   (1 mark)

Irregular verbs

1 a. The horses **are** galloping.   (1 mark)

  b. The donkey **is** eating hay.   (1 mark)

  c. I **am** feeding the animals.   (1 mark)

2 a. I **was** collecting the eggs.   (1 mark)

  b. The hens **were** clucking.   (1 mark)

  c. We **were** working very hard.   (1 mark)

3 a. They **go** to the farm every Saturday.   (1 mark)

  b. She **goes** to her grandparents'
       house every Sunday.   (1 mark)

4 Accept any acceptable sentences, e.g.

  a. He **went** to the park.   (1 mark)

  b. They **went** on holiday to Spain.   (1 mark)

  c. I **went** to school.   (1 mark)

Suffixes

pages 44–45 Which suffix?

1 happy — happily   (1 mark)
   smooth — smoother   (1 mark)
   care — careful   (1 mark)
   enjoy — enjoyment
   sad — sadness   (1 mark)

2 a. help + ? = help**ful**, help**less** or help**er**   (1 mark)

  b. quick + ? = quick**er**, quick**ly** or quick**est** (1 mark)

  c. hope + ? = hope**ful** or hope**less**   (1 mark)

  d. kind + ? = kind**ness**, kind**er**, kind**ly** or kind**est** (1 mark)

  e. fast + ? = fast**er** or fast**est**   (1 mark)

–ly

1 b. slowly   (1 mark)

  c. carefully   (1 mark)

  d. loudly   (1 mark)

  e. thoughtfully   (1 mark)

  f. safely   (1 mark)

–ful

1 "What a **beautiful (1 mark)** place," said Mrs Griffiths.
   "It's **wonderful, (1 mark)** so **peaceful. (1 mark)** It would
   be easy to be **cheerful (1 mark)** every day if I lived here.
   I could keep myself busy doing **useful (1 mark)** things and
   I would stop feeling so **sorrowful. (1 mark)**"
   (Accept alternative answers that still make sense)

Using suffixes

1 a. playful   (1 mark)   b. hopeless   (1 mark)

  c. kindness (1 mark)   d. argument   (1 mark)

  e. nicely   (1 mark)

Homophones

pages 46–47 Sorting homophones

see — sea   (1 mark)
sun — son   (1 mark)
new — knew   (1 mark)
for — four   (1 mark)
read — reed   (1 mark)
through — threw   (1 mark)
blue — blew   (1 mark)
hare — hair   (1 mark)
pear — pair   (1 mark)
one — won   (1 mark)

Which homophone?

1 a. (bee)   (1 mark)   b. (night)   (1 mark)

  c. (pair)   (1 mark)   d. (son)   (1 mark)

  e. (four)   (1 mark)   f. (bear)   (1 mark)

Homophone mix-up!

1 a. The postman delivered the **mail. (1 mark)**

  b. The ball rolled into the **hole. (1 mark)**

  c. Mum read a funny old **tale (1 mark)** to us.

  d. **Where (1 mark)** did you go yesterday?

Homophone horrors!

1 a. They're **(1 mark)**   b. there **(1 mark)**

  c. their **(1 mark)**

2 a. to **(1 mark)** b. too **(1 mark)** c. two **(1 mark)**

Compound, comparative, superlative

pages 48–49 Compound words

1 a. sunset   (1 mark)

  b. whiteboard   (1 mark)

  c. football   (1 mark)

  d. airport   (1 mark)

  e. footprint   (1 mark)

  f. grandmother   (1 mark)

  g. sunflower   (1 mark)

  h. skateboard   (1 mark)

Answers

2 Accept any suitable sentences that use compound words, e.g.
   a. I like big, yellow sunflowers. **(2 marks)**
   b. My teacher writes sums on the whiteboard. **(2 marks)**

Comparative adjectives

1 b. big ⟶ bigger **(1 mark)**
   c. small ⟶ smaller **(1 mark)**
   d. light ⟶ lighter **(1 mark)**
   e. tight ⟶ tighter **(1 mark)**

2 a. faster **(1 mark)**
   b. louder **(1 mark)**

Superlative adjectives

1 b. quickest **(1 mark)** c. shortest **(1 mark)**
   d. darkest **(1 mark)** e. sharpest **(1 mark)**

2 a. nicest! **(1 mark)**
   b. cleverest! **(1 mark)**

Superlative sentences

1 Accept any suitable sentences, e.g.
   b. That ginger kitten is the **cutest** in the litter. **(2 marks)**
   c. Holland is one of the **flattest** countries. **(2 marks)**
   d. That shop is the **littlest** I have ever seen. **(2 marks)**

SATs PRACTICE QUESTIONS

pages 50–54

1 that ✓ **(1 mark)**
2 Accept any suitable answer in the present tense, e.g. eat/have **(1 mark)**
3 Why do we have to wait here – question mark
   I have some new gloves – full stop
   Where is my coat – question mark
   (1 mark for all three correct)
4 Read that book. ✓ **(1 mark)**
5
Put the mess in the bin. — Command
What a day we had! — Exclamation
I've broken a plate. — Question
Can I take another one from the cupboard? — Statement
(1 mark for all three matched correctly)
6 Any suitable answer, e.g. It is the name of a person. **(1 mark)**
7 a comma ✓ **(1 mark)**
8 enjoy**ed** **(1 mark)**
9 If ✓ **(1 mark)**
10 (bright) **(1 mark)**
11 the friendly dog ✓ **(1 mark)**
12 Any suitable answer, e.g. playing **(1 mark)**
13 Any suitable answer, e.g. ran/walked **(1 mark)**
14 What a beautiful star it is! ✓ **(1 mark)**
15 noun ✓ **(1 mark)**
16 lorries – plural
   men – plural
   flag – singular **(1 mark for all three correct)**
17 The flower⊘s in Joe's garden are so colourful. The house⊘s on our street all have lovely garden⊘s.
   (1 mark for all incorrect apostrophes circled)
18 adverb ✓ **(1 mark)**
19 I am
   We have **(1 mark for both correct)**
20 Any suitable answer, e.g. The happy family went on holiday. **(2 marks for an appropriate, grammatically correct sentence, with correct use of capital letters and end punctuation; 1 mark for an appropriate, grammatically correct sentence with incorrect use of capital letters and/or end punctuation)**

Commands and exclamations

❶ Sort and write these sentences into the correct group. **(6 marks)**

How awesome that was!   Choose a book.

What a goal he scored!   Get your coat.

Pay at the till.   What a panic it caused!

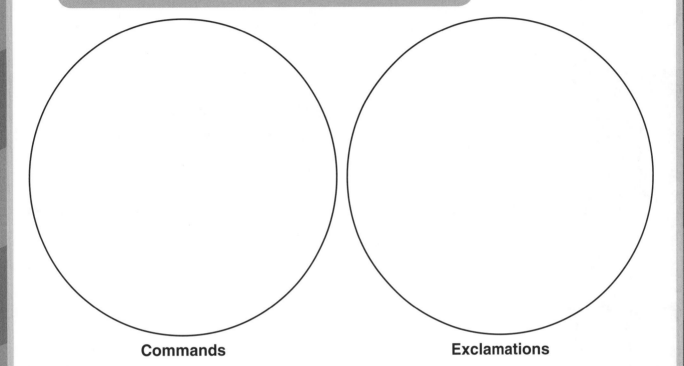

Commands   **Exclamations**

Which is which?

❶ Tick the correct sentence type. **(4 marks)**

Sentence	Question	Exclamation	Command	Statement
Who is that?				
I think it's Zachary.				
Pass me my glasses.				
How good you are!				

Total ── 20

Commas in lists

1 Add the missing commas to these lists.

a. School days: Monday Tuesday Wednesday
Thursday Friday **(1 mark)**

b. Seasons of the year: spring summer autumn winter **(1 mark)**

c. Months in autumn: September October November **(1 mark)**

2 Sort these words into lists. Don't forget your commas!

> a bed   a shower   a fridge   a wardrobe   a bath
> a washing machine   a chest of drawers   a toilet
> a cooker   a lamp   a towel   a kettle

a. Things in a bedroom: .... **(2 marks)**

....

b. Things in a bathroom: .... **(2 marks)**

....

c. Things in a kitchen: .... **(2 marks)**

....

Lists within sentences

1 Add the missing commas to these sentences.

a. In my grandma's garden there is a pond a shed a
bench and lots of beautiful flowers. **(1 mark)**

b. My granddad likes to go for walks watch television read
books and play with me. **(1 mark)**

c. My mum likes swimming reading travelling and going to
the theatre. **(1 mark)**

d. My dad likes hiking reading watching films and going
out with his friends. **(1 mark)**

Writing sentences using commas

1 Make up a sentence for each of these lists.

a. hat   scarf   gloves   coat   (2 marks)

....

....

b. pyjamas   dressing gown   slippers   toothbrush   (2 marks)

....

....

c. lions   giraffes   zebras   hippos   (2 marks)

....

....

2 Write three sentences of your own that include lists.   **(6 marks)**

You can use your own ideas or choose ideas from the box.

holidays	hobbies	food	pets	school	family	friends

a. ....

....

b. ....

....

c. ....

....

Total — 25

Forming contractions

1 Complete this table.

The first one has been done for you.

(14 marks)

Words in Full	Short Form
I am	I'm
it is	
we are	
she had	
cannot	
we will	
does not	
do not	
had not	
would have	
could not	
you are	
he had	
you will	
we have	

Sentences with contractions

1 Choose the correct word to complete each sentence.

can't	I'm	don't	you'll	you're

a. .... going to be late for school. **(1 mark)**

b. My hands are full so .... have to carry your own things. **(1 mark)**

c. I .... walk any faster. **(1 mark)**

d. .... just being lazy! **(1 mark)**

e. .... pull faces at me! **(1 mark)**

Contractions in writing

1 Write the underlined phrases as contractions. **(8 marks)**

Dear Harley,

    <u>I am</u> having a lovely time here in Blackpool. <u>I have</u> been to the funfair, which was great. Tomorrow <u>we are</u> going to the swimming pool and if <u>we have</u> time, <u>we shall</u> picnic on the beach. Next time we come here, <u>you will</u> have to come with us. You <u>would have</u> loved the ice creams we bought on the pier. I <u>could not</u> believe it when a seagull swooped down and ate my dad's chocolate chip cone!

See you soon,
Brooke

a. ....   b. ....   c. ....

d. ....   e. ....   f. ....

g. ....   h. ....

2 Amend the letter by filling in the full version of each word. **(6 marks)**

Dear Mr Goofy,

    <u>You've</u> an appointment with the dentist on Monday 31st October. <u>He'll</u> give you a check-up and tell you if there are any problems. <u>You'll</u> be charged a fee of £15.00 for your visit. Please <u>don't</u> forget to tell us if you <u>can't</u> come to the appointment, otherwise <u>we'll</u> charge you a cancellation fee.

Yours sincerely,

Mr C Dracula (Dental Receptionist)

Dear Mr Goofy,

.... an appointment with the dentist on Monday 31st

October. .... give you a check-up and tell you if there are any

problems. .... be charged a fee of £15.00 for your visit. Please

.... forget to tell us if you .... come to the

appointment, otherwise .... charge you a cancellation fee.

Yours sincerely,

Mr C Dracula (Dental Receptionist)

Total — 33

Apostrophes for belonging

1 Change each sentence to use a possessive apostrophe.

The first one has been done for you.

a. The cup that belongs to Florence ⟶ *Florence's cup*

b. The rattle that belongs to the baby ⟶ .... **(1 mark)**

c. The whiskers that belong to the cat ⟶ .... **(1 mark)**

d. The wings that belong to the butterfly ⟶ .... **(1 mark)**

e. The tail that belongs to the kite ⟶ .... **(1 mark)**

f. The ribbon that belongs to the doll ⟶ .... **(1 mark)**

Yes or no?

1 Are these apostrophes in the correct place? Write **yes** or **no**.

a. Kate's book .... **(1 mark)**

b. Archies' glasses .... **(1 mark)**

c. Hashim's hair .... **(1 mark)**

d. Edies' cake .... **(1 mark)**

e. Mias' ball .... **(1 mark)**

f. James's apple .... **(1 mark)**

Top tip!

Remember, you don't need to add an apostrophe to make a plural. For example, "plums for sale", not "plum's for sale".

What's missing?

❶ Write these phrases out, putting in the missing apostrophes.

a. Ambers dresses .... **(1 mark)**

b. Sallys flowers .... **(1 mark)**

c. The boys shirt .... **(1 mark)**

d. The girls skirt .... **(1 mark)**

e. Jesss jumper .... **(1 mark)**

f. Seans scooter .... **(1 mark)**

Sentences with apostrophes

❶ Put the apostrophe in the correct place, then use each phrase in a sentence.

a. Evies hair **(2 marks)**

....

b. Annies guitar **(2 marks)**

....

c. Nathans computer **(2 marks)**

....

d. Thomass hockey stick **(2 marks)**

....

❷ Are the apostrophes in these sentences correct? Put a ✓ or a ✗ in the boxes.

a. Ben's holiday photo's are great! ☐ **(1 mark)**

b. Karls' camera must be really good. ☐ **(1 mark)**

c. Millie's sandal's look very comfortable. ☐ **(1 mark)**

d. Molly's mum made a fantastic picnic. ☐ **(1 mark)**

Total —— 29

Joining sentences

1 Join the two halves of the sentences together using one of these conjunctions: **and**, **but**, **because**.

a. I do not like bananas .... I love apples. **(1 mark)**

b. I shall finish my homework later ....
I am going to the park now. **(1 mark)**

c. They are going to the park with me ....
they are going to bring a ball. **(1 mark)**

d. We have all brought some money ....
we are going to buy ice cream. **(1 mark)**

Using conjunctions

1 Finish these sentences using your own ideas.

a. Henry worked hard and .... **(1 mark)**

....

b. It is late but .... **(1 mark)**

....

c. They went into town because .... **(1 mark)**

....

d. Ruby has been saving her money because .... **(1 mark)**

....

Choosing conjunctions

1 Rewrite the sentences, joining them with a suitable conjunction.

| or | because | that | when | but |

a. I had to go to the hospital. I was ill. **(1 mark)**

....

b. We went for a walk in the woods. It was raining.   **(1 mark)**

....

c. They decided to stay in the shade. The sun was so hot.   **(1 mark)**

....

d. It was so cold. There were icicles hanging down from the windows.   **(1 mark)**

....

e. We can have milk. We can have water.   **(1 mark)**

....

Co-ordinating or subordinating?

Co-ordinating conjunctions: and   but   or

Subordinating conjunctions: when   because   if   that

❶ Choose the word **subordinating** or **co-ordinating** to describe the conjunction in each sentence.

a. We went to a theme park and we loved it!   **(1 mark)**

....

b. We went on the scariest ride ever but our mum wouldn't join us!   **(1 mark)**

....

c. My dad liked the water slides best because he got very wet.   **(1 mark)**

....

d. I laughed so much when we saw the baboons at the safari park.   **(1 mark)**

....

Total $\frac{}{17}$

Nouns

1 Write these nouns into sets in the correct box. **(3 marks)**

| shorts | paintbrush | trainers |
| spoon | palette | fork |

Cutlery

Clothing

Art equipment

2 Write these nouns into sets in the correct box. **(2 marks)**

| Greece | cheese | king | Shola |

Nouns

Proper nouns

Adjectives

1 Underline the adjective(s) in each sentence.

a. The sugary cakes smelled so sweet! **(2 marks)**

b. The sticky glue was all over the table. **(1 mark)**

c. The excited children ran around the crowded playground. **(2 marks)**

2 Think of suitable adjectives to complete the sentences.

a. The .... teacher waited at the classroom door. **(1 mark)**

b. Our dog has .... fur and

a .... tail. **(2 marks)**

c. There was a .... bang and the room went dark! **(1 mark)**

Adverbs

1 (Circle) the adverb in each sentence.

    a. Ruby danced gracefully across the stage.   **(1 mark)**

    b. Freddie swam smoothly across the pool.   **(1 mark)**

    c. Priya quickly made notes in her book.   **(1 mark)**

    d. Jude leapt athletically into the air.   **(1 mark)**

2 Think of **three** adverbs that can be used with these verbs.

    a. walk .... **(3 marks)**

    b. jump .... **(3 marks)**

    c. sing .... **(3 marks)**

    d. shout .... **(3 marks)**

Verbs

1 Read the passage. (Circle) the verbs.   **(16 marks)**

> Dani loved to bake. Every Saturday afternoon, she took her Grandma's recipe book down off the shelf and chose something to bake. She collected her equipment and gathered her ingredients before she started. She remembered what her Grandma always told her and washed up and tidied as she went along. Today she was trying to make cake pops for the first time. Success! They looked good.

Total $\dfrac{}{46}$

Identifying noun phrases

1 <u>Underline</u> the noun phrase in each sentence.

a. The giant wore huge, clumpy boots.　　　　　**(1 mark)**

b. He had a tangled, messy beard.　　　　　　**(1 mark)**

c. He had an enormous belly.　　　　　　　　**(1 mark)**

d. His fingers were part of his huge, hairy hands.　**(1 mark)**

e. His voice boomed like a big bass drum.　　　**(1 mark)**

f. Spit dribbled from his large, wobbly lips.　　**(1 mark)**

Expanded noun phrases

1 Make a sentence for each of these expanded noun phrases.

a. the little bird that landed on the bird table　　**(2 marks)**

....

....

b. the screaming child who fell off the climbing frame　**(2 marks)**

....

....

c. the tall boy with the curly hair　　　　　　**(2 marks)**

....

....

d. the little girl with the big, red bag　　　　**(2 marks)**

....

....

Writing noun phrases

1 Add two words to each noun to make a noun phrase. The first one has been done for you.

a. a ....*big*..............., ...*blue*............... shoe

b. a ...., ... cat **(1 mark)**

c. a ...., ... chair **(1 mark)**

d. a ...., ... pencil **(1 mark)**

e. a ...., ... surfboard **(1 mark)**

Writing expanded noun phrases

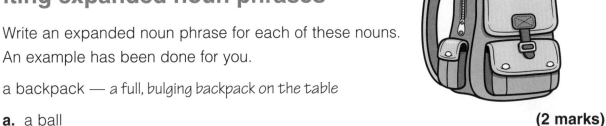

1 Write an expanded noun phrase for each of these nouns. An example has been done for you.

a backpack — *a full, bulging backpack on the table*

a. a ball **(2 marks)**

....

....

b. a hula hoop **(2 marks)**

....

....

c. a bicycle **(2 marks)**

....

....

d. a teddy bear **(2 marks)**

....

....

Total — 26

The present tense

❶ Tick ✓ or cross ✗ if the sentences are correct or incorrect. Rewrite any incorrect sentences. **(4 marks)**

a. She like reading.

b. I cook great pancakes!

c. They play hopscotch.

d. We thinks our teacher is very funny.

....

....

The past tense

❶ Put these verbs into the correct sentence. Use each verb once only.

walked	laughed	jumped	watched	shouted

a. I .... a great film yesterday. **(1 mark)**

b. He .... as high as he could on the trampoline. **(1 mark)**

c. We .... at Isaac's joke. **(1 mark)**

d. She .... across the room. **(1 mark)**

e. They .... quickly into the party. **(1 mark)**

❷ Write a sentence for each of these verbs.

a. kicked **(1 mark)**

....

b. cooked **(1 mark)**

....

c. talked **(1 mark)**

....

d. planted **(1 mark)**

....

–ing endings

1 Add **–ing** to make some new words. **(8 marks)**

a. jump + ing = ...

b. water + ing = ...

c. grow + ing = ...

d. play + ing = ...

e. ride + ing = ...

f. drive + ing = ...

g. like + ing = ...

h. chase + ing = ...

Irregular verbs

1 Choose from: **am   is   are**.

a. The horses .... galloping. **(1 mark)**

b. The donkey .... eating hay. **(1 mark)**

c. I .... feeding the animals. **(1 mark)**

2 Choose from: **was   were**.

a. I .... collecting the eggs. **(1 mark)**

b. The hens .... clucking. **(1 mark)**

c. We .... working very hard. **(1 mark)**

3 Choose from: **go   goes**.

a. They .... to the farm every Saturday. **(1 mark)**

b. She .... to her grandparents' house every Sunday. **(1 mark)**

4 Complete some sentences using the word **went**.

a. He went .... **(1 mark)**

b. They went .... **(1 mark)**

c. I went .... **(1 mark)**

Total $\frac{}{32}$

Which suffix?

1 Draw a line to match the words.
The first one has been done for you.   **(4 marks)**

happy   enjoyment

smooth   sadness

care   careful

enjoy   happily

sad   smoother

2 Add a suffix to each word. Choose from the suffixes below.   **(5 marks)**

> less   ness   er   est   ly   ful

a. help + ? = ...

b. quick + ? = ...

c. hope + ? = ...

d. kind + ? = ...

e. fast + ? = ...

–ly

1 Write each adjective as an adverb. The first one has been done for you.

a. Oliver is a quick runner. He runs .quickly.........................

b. Daisy is a slow reader. She reads .... **(1 mark)**

c. Jack is careful with his work.

   He works .... **(1 mark)**

d. Lottie is a loud singer. She sings .... **(1 mark)**

e. Lily is a thoughtful writer. She writes .... **(1 mark)**

f. Joshua is a safe cyclist. He cycles .... **(1 mark)**

–ful

❶ Choose the correct words to complete the passage.   **(6 marks)**

> beautiful   wonderful   peaceful   sorrowful
> useful   cheerful

"What a .... place," said Mrs Griffiths. "It's ...., so

.... It would be easy to be .... every day if I lived

here. I could keep myself busy doing .... things and I would stop

feeling so ...."

Using suffixes

❶ Use the table to find the correct word for each sentence.

ful	helpful	careful	playful
less	helpless	hopeless	shameless
ly	happily	badly	nicely
ment	enjoyment	argument	amazement
ness	happiness	playfulness	kindness

a. –ful

   My granddad is very .... He enjoys joining in
   our games.   **(1 mark)**

b. –less

   He doesn't like our computer, however. He is ....
   with it!   **(1 mark)**

c. –ness

   My grandma is full of .... and is always thinking
   of others.   **(1 mark)**

d. –ment

   They do not like it when there is an .... between me
   and my sister.   **(1 mark)**

e. –ly

   "Play ....!" they say.   **(1 mark)**

Total ——
25

Sorting homophones

❶ Draw lines to match each pair of homophones. **(10 marks)**

see	won
sun	blew
new	threw
for	hair
read	pair
through	sea
blue	son
hare	knew
pear	four
one	reed

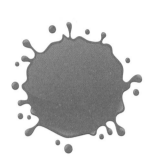

Which homophone?

❶ Read the description, then put a circle around the correct word.

    a. a yellow and black striped insect   **be**   or   **bee**   **(1 mark)**

    b. the opposite of day   **knight**   or   **night**   **(1 mark)**

    c. two things together are often called   **pear**   or   **pair**   **(1 mark)**

    d. my brother is my parents'   **son**   or   **sun**   **(1 mark)**

    e. the number that comes after three   **for**   or   **four**   **(1 mark)**

    f. a large furry animal   **bare**   or   **bear**   **(1 mark)**

Homophone mix-up!

1 Rewrite each sentence with the correct homophone.

a. The postman delivered the male. **(1 mark)**

....

b. The ball rolled into the whole. **(1 mark)**

....

c. Mum read a funny old tail to us. **(1 mark)**

....

d. Wear did you go yesterday? **(1 mark)**

....

Homophone horrors!

1 Choose the correct word to complete the sentences.

> there   their   they're

a. .... very excited about their trip to London. **(1 mark)**

b. You left your coat over ...., by the tree. **(1 mark)**

c. I told them to bring .... roller boots. **(1 mark)**

2 Choose the correct word to complete the sentences.

> two   too   to

a. We went .... Joseph's party. **(1 mark)**

b. He ate .... much cake! **(1 mark)**

c. The party started at .... o'clock. **(1 mark)**

Total $\frac{}{26}$

Compound words

1 Make compound words using the words below.

a. sun + set = ... **(1 mark)**

b. white + board = ... **(1 mark)**

c. foot + ball = ... **(1 mark)**

d. air + port = ... **(1 mark)**

e. foot + print = ... **(1 mark)**

f. grand + mother = ... **(1 mark)**

g. sun + flower = ... **(1 mark)**

h. skate + board = ... **(1 mark)**

2 Write two sentences, using a compound word in each.

a. .... **(2 marks)**

b. .... **(2 marks)**

Comparative adjectives

1 Add **–er** to make a new word.
The first one has been done for you.

a. long ⟶ *longer* ....

b. big ⟶ .... **(1 mark)**

c. small ⟶ .... **(1 mark)**

d. light ⟶ .... **(1 mark)**

e. tight ⟶ .... **(1 mark)**

2 Finish these sentences by using the comparative adjective
in each sentence.

a. My brother is fast but my sister is .... **(1 mark)**

b. That noise was loud but this noise is .... **(1 mark)**

Superlative adjectives

1 Add **–est** to make a new word.
The first one has been done for you.

a. slow slower *slowest* ....

b. quick quicker .... **(1 mark)**

c. short shorter .... **(1 mark)**

d. dark darker .... **(1 mark)**

e. sharp sharper .... **(1 mark)**

2 Finish these sentences.

a. She is nice, he is nicer, I am ....! **(1 mark)**

b. He is clever, she is cleverer, I am ....! **(1 mark)**

Superlative sentences

1 Write a sentence for each of these words.
The first one has been done for you.

a. rude

He is the rudest man I have ever met. ....

b. cute **(2 marks)**

....

c. flat **(2 marks)**

....

d. little **(2 marks)**

....

Total $\frac{}{30}$

1 Tick the correct word to complete the sentence. **(1 mark)**

We go to a bowling alley _____ has a flashing scoreboard.

Tick **one**.

that ☐

when ☐

and ☐

so ☐

2 Write one word on the line below to complete the sentence in the **present tense**. **(1 mark)**

We _____ breakfast at 8 o'clock.

3 Tick to show whether a **question mark** or a **full stop** should complete each sentence. **(1 mark)**

Sentence	Question mark	Full stop
Why do we have to wait here		
I have some new gloves		
Where is my coat		

4 Which sentence is a **command**? **(1 mark)**

Tick **one**.

It is a good book. ☐

I like that book. ☐

Read that book. ☐

Have you read that book? ☐

5 Draw a line to match each sentence to its correct type. **(1 mark)**

One has been done for you.

Sentence		Sentence type
Put the mess in the bin.	——————————	Command
What a day we had!		Exclamation
I've broken a plate.		Question
Can I take another one from the cupboard?		Statement

6 Why does the underlined word start with a capital letter in the sentence below? **(1 mark)**

Mum went shopping and <u>Chloe</u> decided to go too.

....

7 Look where the arrow is pointing. **(1 mark)**

We took sandwiches↑fruit and cake on the picnic.

Which punctuation mark is needed?

Tick **one**.

a question mark ☐

a comma ☐

a full stop ☐

an apostrophe ☐

8 Add a **suffix** to the word <u>enjoy</u> to complete the sentence below. **(1 mark)**

We <u>enjoy____</u> our last summer holiday very much.

9 Tick the correct word to complete the sentence below. **(1 mark)**

_____ you *do* well, you will *get* a prize.

Tick **one**.

If ☐

And ☐

So ☐

Because ☐

10 Circle the **adjective** in the sentence below. **(1 mark)**

The bright light shines across the room.

11 Tick the **noun phrase** below. **(1 mark)**

Tick **one**.

very slowly ☐

had been going ☐

jump over ☐

the friendly dog ☐

12 Write **one** verb to complete what the child is saying. **(1 mark)**

This afternoon, we are _____ in the park.

13 Write one word on the line below to complete the sentence in the **past tense**.   **(1 mark)**

I .... *across the playground to my friends.*

14 Which sentence uses an **exclamation mark** correctly?   **(1 mark)**

Tick **one**.

Did you see that!	☐
Can you see me later!	☐
What a beautiful star it is!	☐
I don't want to see the film!	☐

15 What type of word is underlined in the sentence below?   **(1 mark)**

It was a brilliant <u>show</u>.

Tick **one**.

noun	☐
verb	☐
adjective	☐
adverb	☐

16 Tick to show whether each noun is **singular** or **plural**.   **(1 mark)**

Noun	Singular	Plural
lorries		
men		
flag		

17 Circle the **apostrophes** that are in the wrong places.

One has been done for you.   **(1 mark)**

The flower⓪s in Joe's garden are so colourful.

The house's on our street all have lovely garden's.

18 What type of word is underlined in the sentence below?　**(1 mark)**

The raindrop trickled <u>slowly</u> down the window.

Tick **one**.

adjective ☐

adverb ☐

noun ☐

verb ☐

19 In the table, write in full each of the words with an apostrophe.　**(1 mark)**

One has been done for you.

Words with an apostrophe	Words in full
You've	You have
I'm	
We've	

20 Write **one** sentence to describe something you see in the picture.

Remember to use correct punctuation.　**(2 marks)**

....

Adjective – a word that describes or gives more information about a noun

Adverb – a word that describes or gives more information about an adjective or a verb

Apostrophe – a punctuation mark used to show that something belongs to someone or something; also used to shorten words

Blurb – information about a story found on the back cover of a book

Capital letters – upper-case letters; used at the beginning of a sentence or to start names of people, cities, days of the week and so on

Character – a person or animal in a story

Comma – a punctuation mark used in a list

Comprehension – understanding what you have read

Conjunction – words that join words or phrases

Connective – a 'joining' word, such as a conjunction

Contraction – a word that is made from two words that have been shortened using an apostrophe

Cursive – joined-up handwriting

Deduction – working out clues from a text

Dictionary – a book that explains what words mean

Draft – a first try at a piece of writing

Exclamation mark – a punctuation mark that shows surprise, excitement or something funny

Fiction – imaginary or made up story writing

Full stop – a punctuation mark used at the end of a sentence

Homophones – words that sound the same but are spelt differently and have different meanings

Inference – working out the hidden meaning in a piece of writing

Non-fiction – writing about facts and information that is true

Noun – a word that names a person or thing

Noun phrase – a group of words that work together (one of the words is a noun)

Past tense – a form of a verb for something that has happened

Phonics – using letter sounds to read and write words

Phrase – a group of words

Picture cues – using pictures to help understand what you are reading

Plan – a way to arrange or decide writing ideas

Plot – a plan for a story

Plural – more than one

Prediction – saying what you think will happen

Present tense – form of a verb for something that is happening now

Print – handwriting that is not joined up

Question mark – a punctuation mark used at the end of a sentence that is a question

Recount – a piece of writing that retells an event

Sequence – putting events in order of when they happen

Setting – the time and place where the story is set

Singular – one

Strategies – ways of working something out

Suffix – a group of letters added to the end of a word

Verb – a word for an action

Vocabulary – words that make up a language